# 100 AMAZING FACTS ABOUT CYCLING

Inspirational Stories and Curiosities for kids and young readers

## PRESENTATION

This book is part of the **WORLD STORIES ENCYCLOPEDIA series**, an important editorial project specialized in publications for children and teenagers, and suitable for curious people of all ages.

The series includes various books with a fascinating selection of **incredible stories, facts and curiosities about volleyball, various sports, animals, nature, science.**

All created with the help and advice of **industry experts** to always provide high quality information and content.

The even more attractive thing is that through these books children and teenagers will perfect their cognitive and logical skills simply by having fun.
**What's more beautiful?**

Happy reading and have fun friends.

## The Myth of the Yellow Jersey

The Tour de France is a legendary cycling race that saw the emergence of one of the most iconic symbols in the world of cycling: the yellow jersey. This item of clothing has become the emblem of the race leader, but few know its history.

Way back in 1919, Henri Desgrange, the founder and director of the Tour, introduced the yellow jersey to clearly distinguish the leader of the race, creating an icon of prestige and ambition. This jersey became the tangible symbol of the determination, endurance and ambition of cyclists who face mountains, plains, and many other challenges along the Tour route.

## The Giro d'Italia and its legendary climbs

The Giro d'Italia is much more than just a race. It's an epic adventure that spans breathtaking landscapes and daring challenges. Among the most fearsome and fascinating mountains is the Stelvio Pass, a peak that rises to 2,758 meters above sea level. This epic climb not only tests the cyclists' physical strength, but also their determination and perseverance.

Despite its harshness, the Stelvio Pass continues to exert a magnetic charm on cyclists. It is a test that attracts not only professionals but also cycling lovers, driven by the desire to test themselves on one of the most iconic and legendary climbs in the cycling world. Every cyclist who tackles the Stelvio Pass becomes part of a story of courage and audacity,

## The Finish Line of Paris-Roubaix and Its Legendary Pavés

Paris-Roubaix is known as the "Classic of Stones". Its charm and unique challenge lie in its cobblestone stretches, streets paved with irregular cobblestones.

These segments not only test the endurance of the bikes but also the tenacity of the athletes. Imagine: cyclists tackling these rough and often wet sections, vibrating in every fibre of their body, facing not only a race against their opponents, but also against the stones and challenges of the road itself. Paris-Roubaix is a race of pure courage and determination.

## Cycling as a symbol of freedom and adventure

Cycling is not just a sporting activity, but a symbol of freedom and adventure. Pedalling along endless roads or crossing continents on two wheels offers a feeling of absolute freedom. It's an experience that connects the rider with the surrounding landscape in a way that no other activity can.

The wind on the face, the sight of the places crossed and the feeling of personal conquest create a profound bond between the individual and the world around him, broadening the sense of freedom and adventure, offering unique emotions that only cycling can give.

## The Youngest Winner of the Tour de France

Henri Cornet, by winning the Tour de France in 1904 at less than 20 years old, left an indelible mark on the history of cycling. His victory was extraordinary not only for his young age, but also for the context in which it occurred. The Tour de France was then a gruelling competition, with much longer stages than today and often unpaved roads.

Cornet had to demonstrate not only exceptional cycling ability but also remarkable endurance and tenacity to overcome physical and environmental challenges. His victory anticipated the emergence of young talents in cycling, showing that age is no limit to high-level sporting performance.

**The first women's cycling competitions**

Women's cycling competitions have a rich and sometimes overlooked history. The 1868 race, in addition to being one of the first documented women's sporting events, was a crucial moment for the visibility of women in sport.

These courageous early female cyclists broke the social conventions of the time, challenging perceptions about the role of women in sport and society. Over time, women's competitions have become increasingly popular, leading to wider recognition of female athletes, and contributing to the evolution of cycling as an inclusive sport for all genders.

## The Tour de France and its "Longest Race"

The 1926 stage of the Tour de France, 482 kilometres long, represents a milestone in the history of cycling. Cyclists of that era faced extremely difficult conditions: bad roads, heavy bicycles and without modern technology.

This stage, in addition to its length, was characterized by a significant difference in altitude and often took place in adverse weather conditions. Overcoming such a challenge required extraordinary physical and mental endurance, as well as tactical ability to face the long hours of competition. This event not only tested human limits but also helped shape the Tour de France as one of the most difficult and prestigious sporting competitions in the world.

## The Most Expensive Bicycle in the World

The most expensive bicycle in the world is an extraordinary example of how the passion for cycling can meet art and luxury. This bicycle, adorned with gold and diamonds, represents a unique combination of functionality and aesthetics.

Despite its practical uselessness in competition or everyday use, it serves as a symbol of status and craftsmanship excellence. Its creation requires high expertise in various fields, from metallurgy to jewellery, demonstrating how cycling can inspire works that go beyond simple transportation.

## The Influence of Cycling on Cities

The impact of cycling on modern cities is tangible and ever-growing. The increase in cycling infrastructure in cities such as Amsterdam, Copenhagen and many others has demonstrated how cycling can be an effective solution to traffic and pollution problems. This change not only improves air quality and reduces noise, but also promotes a healthier lifestyle.

Cycling cities tend to be more liveable, with a stronger sense of community and more equitable and accessible urban space. Additionally, adopting cycling as a primary mode of transportation can have a positive impact on the local economy by reducing road infrastructure costs and stimulating commerce in urban neighbourhoods.

## The importance of nutrition in cycling

In the world of cycling, nutrition is a crucial aspect. During a demanding race like the Tour de France, a professional cyclist can burn up to 6,000-7,000 calories a day.

Maintaining adequate nutrition and hydration is essential to support endurance and performance during such a gruelling competition. Cyclists follow rigorous nutritional plans to ensure a constant energy supply and correct recovery after each stage.

## The feat of Everesting by bicycle

Everesting by bicycle is an extreme challenge that is gaining popularity among cycling enthusiasts. Cyclists must repeat an uphill route until they reach a total height difference of 8,848 metres, the equivalent of the altitude of Everest.
This feat requires not only exceptional physical endurance, but also strong mental determination.

The choice of climb, the repetition strategy, and nutrition during the challenge are all crucial aspects to plan carefully. Everesting represents not only a physical challenge but also a personal journey of self-determination, with cyclists facing physical and mental limits in a test of pure endurance.

## The Birth of the Mountain Bike

The origins of mountain biking date back to the 1970s in Marin County, California, where a group of avid cyclists began modifying their road bikes to adapt to rugged terrain and mountain trails.

These pioneers experimented with sturdier frames, wider tires, and more effective braking systems, creating a bicycle suited to difficult terrain.

Their work revolutionized cycling, introducing a more dynamic and adventurous riding style. Mountain biking has opened up new horizons in the world of cycling, making it possible to explore unexplored terrain and stimulating the development of new cycling technologies.

## The Bikepacking Phenomenon

Bikepacking combines cycling and camping, offering a unique experience of exploration and adventure. Cyclists load their bikes with lightweight camping gear, food, and necessary tools, and embark on journeys through diverse landscapes.

This travel mode promotes sustainability and independence, allowing cyclists to fully immerse themselves in nature. Bikepacking has developed not only as a sport, but also as a lifestyle, attracting people looking to disconnect from everyday life and connect with their surroundings in a more intimate and adventurous way.

## The Mystery of the "Ghost Bikes"

The "ghost bikes" are a touching tribute to fallen cyclists. These memorials, often painted white and placed at accident sites, serve as a solemn reminder of the danger's cyclists face on the roads.

These silent but powerful installations aim to raise public awareness of road safety, encouraging motorists and cyclists to share the road respectfully and safely. The presence of a "ghost bike" is a visual reminder that incites reflection and highlights the importance of road policies and infrastructure that protect all road users.

## The Rise of Track Cycling Competitions

Track cycling is an exciting and intense cycling discipline. These races take place in velodromes with oval tracks, generally made of wood, which offer a smooth and fast surface. Competitions vary from speed tests, such as sprinting, to endurance tests, such as individual pursuit or points racing. Track cyclists must possess a unique combination of power, speed, tactical ability, and precision in bike control.

This discipline requires not only intense physical preparation but also acute tactical awareness, as races are often decided by fractions of a second.

Track cycling offers a fascinating, high-speed spectacle that continues to gain popularity.

### The bicycle as a tool for social change

Bicycles have been used as tools of social change in many parts of the world.

Programs that provide bicycles to disadvantaged communities or to those who need them to get to work or schools are helping to improve accessibility and mobility, transforming the lives of many people, and opening up opportunities for growth and development.

## The Culture of "Critical Mass"

"Critical Mass" is a cycling movement involving groups of cyclists who gather periodically in many cities around the world to celebrate cycling and raise awareness of the importance of this sustainable means of transport.

These rallies aim to promote awareness of cycling as an ecological and healthy way to get around the city.

## The "Group B" Phenomenon in Cycling

"Group B" is a term used in professional cycling to identify the group of cyclists who find themselves outside of the fight for victory in a race.

These riders can work together to finish the race or to help each other in the less competitive phases of the competition, demonstrating the sense of camaraderie and support present in the world of cycling.

## The role of bicycles in wars

During the First World War, bicycles were used by troops as fast and practical means of transport. Bicycles proved useful for couriers and scouts, providing a quick and efficient way to move around the battlefield, demonstrating the importance of this vehicle even in conflict situations.

## The eclectic world of vintage bicycles

The world of vintage bicycles is a fascinating universe for enthusiasts. Collecting and restoring vintage bikes has become a popular hobby.

Historic bicycles not only represent a cultural heritage but also testify to the evolution of design and technology over the decades, arousing admiration for their beauty and the story they tell.

## Cycling and the link with Environmental Sustainability

Cycling is considered one of the most environmentally friendly ways to get around. Using the bicycle as a means of transport reduces greenhouse gas emissions and air pollution, thus contributing to the preservation of the environment.

This form of sustainable mobility plays a crucial role in the fight against climate change by encouraging the reduction of carbon emissions in cities.

**Cycling as a form of artistic expression**

The world of cycling has inspired artists of various disciplines. From works of art celebrating the beauty of bicycles and racing, to performances by street artists who use two wheels as elements in their shows, cycling has transformed into a form of artistic expression, integrating the passion for cycling in contemporary creative culture.

## The Social Impact of Cycling-Related Charities

Several charities have developed around cycling, using the sport as a means of raising money for social causes.

Charity rides, fundraising events and cycling marathons have become effective ways to raise awareness and funds for medical research, to support disadvantaged communities or to promote education and health.

## Innovation in Bicycle Design

Bicycle design continues to evolve, combining aesthetics and functionality. Cycling companies invest in the research and development of new materials and frame geometries, creating bicycles that offer superior performance, optimal comfort, and greater durability. Attention to detail in bicycle design has paved the way for a more enjoyable and efficient riding experience.

### Cycling as a tool for social inclusion

Cycling has become a means to promote social inclusion. Projects and initiatives promote cycling as a tool for inclusion for people with disabilities, offering adaptations and technical support to allow everyone to enjoy the benefits of cycling.

These programs demonstrate how cycling can break down barriers and foster a sense of community and equality.

## The Legend of Fausto Coppi and the Duel with Gino Bartali

Fausto Coppi is one of the greatest cyclists in history, known for his charisma and extraordinary talent. His epic duel with Gino Bartali marked a golden era of Italian cycling.

During the 1949 Giro d'Italia, Coppi and Bartali competed in one of the most intense rivalries in the history of the sport, with Bartali fighting tenaciously while Coppi proved unstoppable. This epic duel ended with Coppi's victory, leaving an indelible mark on the history of the Giro d'Italia and world cycling.

## Tom Simpson's Heroic Victory at the 1965 World Cup

Tom Simpson is remembered for his epic victory at the 1965 World Championship in San Sebastián, Spain.

In a harsh and exhausting race, under extreme heat, Simpson proved to be tenacious and determined, resisting his opponents and the effort to win the world title.

Sadly, his career was marred by a tragic death during the Tour de France in 1967, but his World Championship victory remains an iconic moment in cycling.

## Bernard Hinault: The Breton of the Tour de France

Bernard Hinault, known as "The Breton ", for his indomitable character and tenacity, is a legendary figure in the world of cycling, particularly in the Tour de France. His career, marked by competitive aggression and an iron will, saw him win five Tours de France (1978, 1979, 1981, 1982 and 1985).

Hinault stood out not only for his physical abilities, but also for his tactical astuteness, a quality that allowed him to dominate in the most critical phases of racing. His duel with Greg LeMond in the 1986 Tour became a symbol of his determination: despite a strong rivalry with his American teammate, Hinault showed extraordinary resilience, fighting until the end for the yellow jersey.

## Miguel Indurain: The Silent Dominator of the Tour

In the Tour de France landscape, Miguel Indurain emerges as an imposing figure for his achievements in the 1990s. Known for his measured racing style and phenomenal time trial ability, Indurain set an incredible record by winning five consecutive editions of the Tour (1991 to 1995).

This series of victories, achieved thanks to a unique combination of power, endurance, and race management, marked an era in cycling. Indurain was a master at maintaining control in mountain stages and dominating in time trials, demonstrating superior physical conditioning and impeccable concentration. His reign in the Tour de France is remembered as one of the most dominant periods in cycling history.

### Gino Bartali: The Hero Cyclist

Gino Bartali is not only a legend of Italian cycling for his victories in the Tour de France (1938 and 1948) and other great races, but also a hero for his courage and humanity during the Second World War. Using his position as a renowned cyclist, Bartali played a crucial role in saving Jews from Nazi persecution by carrying false documents hidden in the frame of his bicycle.

This heroic act, performed at great personal risk, helped save hundreds of lives and earned him recognition as "Righteous Among the Nations." In the world of cycling, Bartali is remembered for his incredible resilience, his fighting spirit, and his profound humanity, becoming a symbol of courage both on a bicycle and in life.

**Eddy Merckx: The King of the Triple Crown**
Eddy Merckx, nicknamed the "Cannibal" for his insatiable thirst for victories, set numerous cycling records, including the historic "Triple Corona" in 1974. This title, one of the most difficult and rare to obtain, was the result of Merckx's victory in the Giro d'Italia, the Tour de France and the World Championship in the same year.

This feat highlighted his extraordinary versatility as a cyclist, capable of excelling in different types of races, from mountains to time trials, from classics to major stage races. His career, characterized by near-total dominance in the races he participated in, cemented his position as one of the greatest cyclists of all time.

### Felice Gimondi: A Versatile Champion

Felice Gimondi stands out in the history of cycling for his exceptional versatility and successes in major stage races. One of the few cyclists to win all three Grand Tours (Giro d'Italia, Tour de France and Vuelta a España), Gimondi has demonstrated a unique ability to adapt to different types of racing and challenges.

His victory at the Tour de France in 1965, on his debut, stunned the cycling world and marked the beginning of a career full of triumphs. Known for his ability to compete in both mountains and time trials, Gimondi left an indelible mark on cycling, becoming an example of multifaceted talent and lasting success.

## Paper Bicycles and the Giro d'Italia in the Second World War

During the years of the Second World War, Italy, like many other European countries, was deeply affected by the lack of resources. This situation also had a significant impact on the world of cycling. In those years, there was a serious shortage of metal, necessary for the production of bicycles, due to its reallocation for the war efforts. This led to the innovative creation of bicycles made largely of pressed paper and wood.

The 1946 Giro, the first after the end of the war, was particularly emblematic. Although the resource situation had improved somewhat, many cyclists still used pressed paper bicycles. This edition of the Giro was a symbol of hope and rebirth for war-ravaged Italy.

## The rivalry between Jacques Anquetil and Raymond Poulidor

Jacques Anquetil and Raymond Poulidor created one of the most famous rivalries in French cycling. Anquetil was known for his coolness and his skill in the backbeat, while Poulidor was loved by the public for his humility and his courage in the climbs. Their rivalry, with epic clashes during the Tour de France, has become legendary in the history of French cycling.

# 35

## Stephen Roche and the Triumph of 1987

In 1987, Stephen Roche achieved an extraordinary feat in cycling, joining an exclusive club of champions. In that year, Roche won the Giro d'Italia, the Tour de France and the World Championship, a trio of victories that very few cyclists in history have managed to achieve.

His victory in the Giro d'Italia was marked by extraordinary determination and tactics, where he had to face not only fierce opponents, but also the challenges of adverse weather conditions and difficult mountain climbs.

At the Tour de France, Roche showed incredible endurance, especially in the famous La Plagne stage, where he made up a gap that seemed insurmountable. His victory at the World Championships completed a year of unprecedented triumphs.

## 36

**Marco Pantani: The Heroic Victory of 1998**

Marco Pantani, nicknamed "The Pirate" for his aggressive style and unmistakable image, etched his name into the history of the Giro d'Italia with an epic victory in 1998. His feat was particularly memorable in the Passo di Mortirolo, one of the hardest climbs in world cycling.

Starting with a significant disadvantage, Pantani made a phenomenal climb, demonstrating not only physical superiority, but also great mental strength. He overtook his opponents one after another, making up for lost time and gaining a decisive lead.

# 37

## Jacques Anquetil vs Raymond Poulidor: An Epic Duel

The confrontation between Jacques Anquetil and Raymond Poulidor at the Tour de France in the 1960s represents one of the most intense and memorable rivalries in the history of cycling. Anquetil, known for his elegant style and mastery of time trials, and Poulidor, loved for his tenacity and popular appeal, faced each other in a series of thrilling duels.

This rivalry reached its peak in 1964, particularly on the stage up the Puy de Dôme, where the two engaged in a wheel-to-wheel battle, with Poulidor desperately trying to break away from Anquetil. Anquetil narrowly maintained his lead, securing the Tour victory.

## The 1989 World Championship and Greg LeMond's victory

The 1989 World Championships saw one of the most incredible finishes in cycling history. Greg LeMond and Laurent Fignon battled in an epic time trial, with Fignon taking the lead on the final day of the race.

However, LeMond adopted an innovative aerodynamic position, using aero handlebars to reduce wind resistance, gaining a crucial advantage, and winning the World Championship by just eight seconds, thus confirming his skill and determination.

# 39

## The "Campionissimo" Fausto Coppi and his Unparalleled Charisma

Fausto Coppi was one of the greatest cyclists in history, famous for his charisma and extraordinary talent.

He won the Giro d'Italia five times, the Tour de France twice and the World Championship once. His elegant style in the saddle and his skill in climbing have made him an immortal icon of Italian and world cycling.

# 40

## The rivalry between Felice Gimondi and Eddy Merckx at the Giro d'Italia

Felice Gimondi and Eddy Merckx fuelled an epic rivalry during the Giro d'Italia. Gimondi, known for his consistency and cunning, and Merckx, considered one of the best cyclists of all time, faced each other in fierce competition during several editions of the race.

This rivalry has captured the imagination of cycling fans and helped create some of the most exciting challenges in the history of the Giro.

# 41

## Stephen Roche's Heroic Victory at the 1987 Giro d'Italia

Stephen Roche achieved a legendary victory in the 1987 Giro d'Italia.

After an exhausting and hard-fought race, Roche overcame his rivals with determination and courage, conquering the Giro and becoming the second cyclist, after Merckx, to win the Giro d'Italia, the Tour de France and the World Championship in the same year.

# 42

## The Legend of Gino Bartali and his Courage during the Second World War

Gino Bartali was a hero both on the roads and outside of cycling. During World War II, Bartali hid false documents inside the frame of his bicycle to help Jews escape Nazi persecution.

His courage and humanity helped save many lives, making him an icon of courage and altruism, as well as a cycling legend.

# 43

## The Tragic Fate of Tommy Simpson at the 1967 Tour de France

Tommy Simpson, a talented British cyclist, lost his life during the 1967 Tour de France. During the stage on Mount Ventoux, facing extreme temperatures and his gruelling effort, Simpson collapsed and died due to a mix of physical exhaustion and use of stimulants.

His death highlighted the dangers of stimulant substance abuse in professional cycling, leading to changes in policy and awareness of the risks of drug use in sport.

# 44

## The Epic Duel between Greg LeMond and Laurent Fignon at the 1989 Tour de France

The 1989 Tour de France was characterized by an exciting duel between Greg LeMond and Laurent Fignon.

In the final stage, a time trial in Paris, LeMond, using aerodynamic handlebars as an innovation, managed to win by just eight seconds, making one of the most incredible comebacks in the history of the Tour, taking the yellow jersey and the title.

# 45

## The "Escape of the Champions" at the 1949 Giro d'Italia

The 1949 Giro d'Italia entered history for the "Escape of the Champions", an epic episode which saw Gino Bartali and Fausto Coppi, two of the greatest legends of Italian cycling, as protagonists. Their rivalry, known to all fans, reached a climax during the seventeenth stage, from Cuneo to Pinerolo.

In this stage, Bartali and Coppi unexpectedly formed a temporary alliance, deciding to work together to distance themselves from the other riders. Their escape began in the first kilometres and turned into a breathtaking race through the Alps, tackling legendary passes such as Maddalena, Vars, Izoard, Montgenevre and Sestriere.

## 46

## Peter Sagan and his record in the Road Cycling World Championships

Peter Sagan, one of the most charismatic and versatile cyclists of his time, made cycling history by winning three consecutive titles in the Road Cycling World Championship (2015, 2016, 2017).

This extraordinary achievement not only highlighted his consistency and ability in different types of racing, but also established Sagan as one of the greatest talents in world cycling. His ability to excel in sprints, classics and hill climb races makes him a unique cyclist, capable of competing and winning in almost any type of race.

His victory in 2017, in particular, was a display of strength and tactical astuteness, confirming his position as one of the most complete and admired cyclists of his time.

# 47

## Chris Froome and the 2013 Tour de France

In 2013, Chris Froome conquered the Tour de France in impressive fashion, emerging as a new dominator in road cycling. His performance in that edition was characterized by exceptional skill in the climbs and time trials.

Froome took command of the race in the first mountain stages, demonstrating an almost indisputable superiority over his rivals. His victory was not only the result of his physical strength, but also of his tactical intelligence and his ability to manage the race.

This triumph marked the start of a successful era for Froome in the Tour de France, cementing him as one of modern cycling's greatest climbers and time trialists.

## Alfredo Binda: Pioneer and Legend of the Giro d'Italia

Alfredo Binda, a name that resonates in the history of the Giro d'Italia, was one of the race's first great champions. Winning the Giro five times (1925, 1927, 1928, 1929 and 1933), Binda demonstrated almost absolute superiority, dominating the mountain stages and the time trials. His technique, his climbing ability and his endurance made him almost unbeatable in those years, establishing the model for future cycling champions.

In addition to his Giro victories, Binda had a significant impact on the development and popularity of cycling in Italy, helping to elevate the Giro d'Italia into one of the country's most prestigious sporting events. His legacy is not limited to his victories, but also includes his contribution to improving technique and tactics in cycling.

# 49

## Vincenzo Nibali's revenge at the 2016 Giro d'Italia

Vincenzo Nibali's victory in the 2016 Giro d'Italia was a demonstration of pure grit and resilience.

During the race, Nibali found himself facing multiple challenges, including a less than ideal start and strong competition from rivals. However, in the second half of the Giro, he began a remarkable comeback. His ability in the descents and mountain stages came to the fore in the latter stages of the race, especially in the Alpine stage with the arrival in Risoul, where he made a breathtaking descent that turned the tide of the race.

Nibali demonstrated not only his technical superiority, but also incredible mental strength, overtaking his opponents one after the other and taking the pink jersey in the penultimate stage.

# 50

## Marianne Vos: The Dominatrix of Women's Cycling

Marianne Vos is widely recognized as one of the most versatile and successful cyclists of all time.

His career is characterized by an impressive number of victories in various cycling disciplines, including road cycling, track cycling and cyclocross. Vos has won numerous World Championships and major races in road cycling, demonstrating an ability to compete and win in every type of race. Her agility, power and tactical intelligence have made her a dominant figure in women's cycling, inspiring a generation of cyclists.

# 51

## Anna van der Breggen and the 2020 Women's Giro d'Italia

Anna van der Breggen marked her era in women's cycling with a memorable victory at the Giro d'Italia Femminile in 2020. Demonstrating undeniable superiority, particularly in the mountain stages, van der Breggen took command of the race with authority and determination .

His victory was the result of a combination of physical strength, endurance, and tactical cunning.

Her ability to manage the race and attack at the right time demonstrated her status as one of the strongest cyclists on the world scene, confirming her versatility and talent in different types of racing.

# 52

## Johan Museeuw's emotional farewell to the 2002 Tour of Flanders

Johan Museeuw, nicknamed "The Lion of Flanders", ended his career in 2002 with a final, emotional participation in the Tour of Flanders.

Museeuw, a true cycling legend, particularly in the Northern Classics, chose this race, which he had won three times previously, for his retirement. Although he didn't win, his final race was a tribute to his incredible career.

Along the route, fans paid tribute to Museeuw with applause and standing ovations, recognizing his significant contribution to cycling and celebrating his many victories and fighting spirit.

# 53

## The Legend of Beryl Burton, Queen of the Golden Era of Women's Cycling

Beryl Burton was one of Britain's greatest female cyclists. In the 1960s and 1970s, it dominated road and track cycling.

Her extraordinary skill led her to beat even her male opponents, setting world records that remained unbeaten for decades. Her impact on women's cycling has been remarkable, paving the way for the growth and recognition of women in the cycling world.

**54**

## The Tour de France during the First World War

During the First World War, the Tour de France continued despite the challenges. Although the 1915-1918 editions were not held due to the war conflict, the Tour resumed in 1919, becoming a symbol of rebirth and hope, helping to unite the nation after the horrors of war.

# 55

## The Contribution of Cycling to Scientific Research

Cycling has often been used as a means of collecting scientific data. Several professional cycling teams have collaborated with research institutions to monitor athletic performance, training, and the impact of exercise on the human body.

These studies have helped develop knowledge and technologies to improve the performance and health of cyclists.

# 56

## The History of the Pink Jersey of the Giro d'Italia

The pink jersey, symbol of the leader in the general classification of the Giro d'Italia, was introduced in 1931.

The colour pink was chosen because the newspaper La Gazzetta dello Sport, organizer of the Giro, printed its pages on pink paper. This jersey has become an icon in the world of cycling, representing leadership and exceptionalism while racing.

## "Solidarity cycling" and charity rides

Benefit rides have become a phenomenon in the cycling world. Events like "Bike MS" and "Ride for the Roses" involve cyclists of all abilities to raise money for disease research and to support humanitarian causes.

These events demonstrate how cycling can be an effective means of promoting solidarity and charity.

# 58

## The Role of the First Bicycles in the Struggle for Women's Rights

In the late 19th century, bicycles played a crucial role in the emancipation of women. The use of bicycles allowed women to gain greater autonomy and freedom of movement, contributing to the fight for gender equality and their more active participation in society.

# 59

## "Ageless Cycling" and Physical Activity for the Elderly

Cycling is an accessible physical activity even for the elderly. Initiatives such as "Ageless Cycling" engage older adults on bicycles, allowing them to enjoy the benefits of physical activity while maintaining their health and independence.

**60**

## The Role of Bicycles in Environmental Conservation

Electric bicycles are becoming an increasingly popular choice for reducing pollution. With rechargeable batteries and a smaller carbon footprint than motor vehicles, e-bikes are emerging as a sustainable alternative for urban mobility.

# 61

## The Milan-Sanremo Race and the "Cipressa" Challenge

The Milan-Sanremo, one of the classic monuments of cycling, is known for its spectacular and challenging route. One of the key elements is the Cipressa climb, which precedes the famous final climb to Poggio. La Cipressa was the scene of memorable attacks, often influencing the final outcome of the race.

# 62

## The "Sormano Wall" at the Giro di Lombardia

The Giro di Lombardia features one of the most challenging sections of cycling: the "Sormano Wall". This extremely steep and demanding climb, with gradients exceeding 25%, tests the endurance and determination of cyclists, making this stage one of the most feared and fascinating of the race.

## 63

**The rivalry between Fabian Cancellara and Tom Boonen in the Pavé Classics**

Fabian Cancellara and Tom Boonen have long challenged in cobbled classics such as Paris-Roubaix and the Tour of Flanders. Their epic battles on these rugged and rutted roads, known for their distinctive cobblestones, enchanted enthusiasts, becoming a legendary chapter in the history of the classics.

# 64

## The Giro Rosa and the Affirmation of Women's Cycling

The Giro Rosa, also known as the Giro d'Italia Femminile, represents the pinnacle of women's cycling worldwide.

This competition, which began in the 1980s, has over time acquired a prestige and importance equal to that of its male counterpart. The participating female cyclists tackle extremely challenging stages, including difficult climbs and time trials, displaying a level of skill, endurance and determination that is in no way inferior to their male colleagues.

The Giro Rosa has become a fundamental event for promoting and enhancing women's cycling, offering athletes a platform to demonstrate their talent and strength. This race significantly contributed to raising the status of women's cycling.

## The Climb of Alpe d'Huez and Its Legends

Alpe d'Huez, also known as "The Island of the Sun", is one of the most emblematic and feared climbs in the world of cycling. Located in the French Alps, this climb is famous for its 21 hairpin bends, each named after a Tour de France stage winner.

The climb has become a place of worship for cycling enthusiasts, famous for its steep gradients and the unique atmosphere created by the fans along the route. The memorable clashes and heroic victories on these ramps have helped create the legend of Alpe d'Huez, making it one of the most anticipated and spectacular stages of the Tour.

## Cycling as a Means of Exploration and Adventure

Cycling goes far beyond sporting competition; it's also an amazing medium for exploration and adventure.

Adventure cyclists from all over the world have used the bicycle to undertake incredible journeys, crossing breathtaking landscapes and different cultures. These feats, ranging from long continental crossings to expeditions in extreme environments, demonstrate the versatility of the bicycle as a means of travel and the ability of cyclists to overcome physical and mental challenges.

These bicycle trips offer not only a unique perspective on the world, but also a profound experience of personal growth and connection with nature.

# 67

## The Tour Down Under and the Opening of the Cycling Season

The Tour Down Under, which takes place in Australia, has the privilege of opening the professional road cycling season. As the first UCI WorldTour event, the Tour Down Under attracts some of the world's best cyclists, who compete in a series of stages across the unique landscapes of South Australia.

The race, typically held in January, is known for its weather challenges, with the Australian summer heat adding an extra layer of difficulty. As well as being a major sporting event, the Tour Down Under is also a major festival for cycling enthusiasts, with side events and parties attracting large audiences, celebrating the start of the international cycling season.

# 68

## Cycling as a Symbol of Resilience and Redemption: The Story of Nelson Vails

The story of Nelson Vails, nicknamed "Cheetah", is an emblematic example of how cycling can be a symbol of resilience and redemption.

Growing up in a difficult environment in Harlem, New York, Vails found cycling as an escape from the challenges of everyday life. His incredible rise in the world of track cycling has been a demonstration of pure determination and talent. Initially working as a bicycle courier, Vails honed his cycling skills in an intense and competitive urban context.

His career culminated in winning the silver medal at the 1984 Olympics in Los Angeles, an achievement that marked a historic moment in cycling.

## 69

## Bicycle Culture in the Netherlands and Denmark

The Netherlands and Denmark are renowned for their advanced cycling culture. In these countries, the bicycle is not just a means of transport, but an integral part of lifestyle and urban planning.

The dense network of cycle paths, safe and accessible infrastructure, and consideration of cycling in urban policies have made these nations role models globally. In cities such as Amsterdam and Copenhagen, cycling is the preferred means of transport for a large segment of the population, thanks to its ease of access, convenience and reduced environmental impact.

This cycling culture is also reflected in strong government support, with policies aimed at promoting cycling and reducing dependence on cars.

# 70

## Jeannie Longo's Record in the Women's Time Trial

Jeannie Longo is one of the most influential and successful figures in women's cycling. His outstanding career was marked by numerous victories, particularly in time trials.

Longo dominated the French Time Trial Championship, winning it 13 times, a record that testifies not only to his extraordinary cycling ability, but also to his incredible longevity and consistency over time. In addition to his national successes, Longo has also achieved important results at an international level, winning world championships and successfully participating in several Olympics.

# 71

## The "Tour of the Dolomites" and the Spectacular Mountain Roads

The Giro delle Dolomiti is a cycling event that attracts enthusiasts from all over the world for its scenic beauty and technical challenges. This granfondo allows cyclists to immerse themselves in the majestic mountains of the Dolomites, a UNESCO heritage site, offering routes that wind through spectacular mountain scenery.

The race includes some of the most famous and challenging passes, such as the Stelvio Pass and the Giau Pass, testing the skill and endurance of the participants. In addition to the sporting aspect, the Giro delle Dolomiti is also a cultural experience, allowing cyclists to explore the rich traditions of Italy's Alpine regions.

# 72

## Francesco Moser's Hour Record

Francesco Moser, famous Italian cyclist of the 70s and 80s, is remembered for his extraordinary hour record. On January 19, 1984, Moser attempted to break the hour record in Mexico City.

Using a specially designed bicycle and an aerodynamic helmet, Moser pedals at constant top speed for a full hour, defying the human limit. The final result is 51.151 km, setting a new hour record.

This feat established him as one of the greatest cyclists of all time and demonstrated his commitment, dedication, and technical preparation to achieve a result of this magnitude.

# 73

## The Road Cycling World Championship and the History of its Symbols

The Road Cycling World Championship, inaugurated in 1927, has seen the emergence and consolidation over time of some significant symbols that embody the spirit and history of this prestigious competition. The best known of these is undoubtedly the rainbow jersey, awarded to the winner of the championship.

This jersey, characterized by horizontal bands of different colours (red, yellow, black, green and light blue) on a white background, represents not only victory in the world championship, but also excellence and prestige in the world of cycling. Beyond the jersey, the World Championship is known for its spirit of internationality and competition at the highest level, with cyclists from all over the world competing in a tactical and physical battle to win the title.

# 74

## The "Giro della Lombardia" and its Autumn Challenges

The Giro della Lombardia, also known as "the Classic of dead leaves", is one of the five classic monuments of cycling and is famous for its autumn event, typically in October.

This race, which passes through the picturesque Lombardy region of Italy, is famous for its unique difficulties: challenging routes that include steep climbs, technical descents, and often uncertain and changeable autumn weather conditions.

The beauty of the landscape, with the warm colours of the autumn leaves, offers a spectacular backdrop to the competition, which requires cyclists not only great endurance and skill in climbing, but also a high ability to adapt to climatic conditions and variations in terrain.

## 75

## The Role of Teams in Professional Cycling and Race Tactics

Professional cycling is based on the organization of teams and their racing tactics. Each team has a mix of specialized riders, such as climbers, sprinters, and long distance runners, with a common goal: for their leader to win.

During big races, teams work together to control the race, protect the leader, and plan strategies to use race conditions to their advantage. Tactics include attacking, covering rivals' attacks, using the psychological aspect and cooperation between teammates to achieve maximum results. This tactical game makes cycling a fascinating and unpredictable sport.

## The Phenomenon of "Road Cycling" and the Varieties of Racing

Road cycling encompasses a wide range of races, from monument classics such as the Giro d'Italia and Tour de France to one-day races such as Paris-Roubaix and Liège-Bastogne-Liège. Each race has its own unique character, with diverse routes that test cyclists' skills and endurance.

Stage races, like the Giro d'Italia, require a combination of climbing skills, time trailing and endurance, while monument classics feature challenging terrain and special features, such as cobbled sections or iconic climbs, which make the competition even more challenging .

## The Impact of Technological Innovation in Bicycles and Equipment

Technological innovation has revolutionized the design and performance of bicycles and cycling equipment. The introduction of advanced materials such as carbon fibre has made bikes lighter, stiffer, and more aerodynamic, improving the performance of racers.

Modern racing bicycles are equipped with electronic transmission and braking systems, more efficient wheels and geometries designed to maximize aerodynamic efficiency. Cycling clothing, such as racing suits and helmets, has also undergone continuous evolution, offering comfort, aerodynamics and protection to professionals during races.

## The Growth of Cycling as a Global Phenomenon and International Racing

Cycling has become a global phenomenon with an ever-widening following in many parts of the world. International races such as the Tour de France and the Giro d'Italia have contributed to the spread of the sport, attracting large audiences, and inspiring a growing number of people to cycle.

Increased participation in cycling events, granfondos, amateur races and interest in electric or hybrid bikes have highlighted the expansion of cycling as a movement involving people of all ages and experience levels.

## Commitment to Cycling for Charity and Social Change

Cycling has proven to be a powerful medium for charity and social change. Several organizations, such as "Bikes for Africa" or "World Bicycle Relief", have used bicycles as a tool to improve access to education, healthcare, and work in disadvantaged communities.

Even through fundraising events such as charity rides or awareness-raising initiatives, cycling has shown that it can have a positive impact on society, promoting solidarity and support for important causes.

## The Importance of Cycling in Italian Culture

Cycling plays a significant role in Italian culture. The country has a long tradition in professional cycling and is the stage for some of the most prestigious races in the world, such as the Giro d'Italia and classics such as Milan-Sanremo.

Cycling is an integral part of everyday life and Italian sporting culture, with thousands of enthusiasts and fans fervently following the races, supporting local riders, and celebrating their success.

## 81

**The Giro d'Italia and its centenary history**

The Giro d'Italia, inaugurated in 1909, is more than just a cycling race: it is an event that embodies the history, culture, and spirit of Italy. For over a century, this stage race has crossed not only the magnificent Italian countryside and imposing mountains, but also cities full of history and art, becoming a symbol of cycling and the beauty of the country.

The Giro is famous for its difficult stages, particularly the ascents in the Dolomites and the Alps, which made cycling legends such as Fausto Coppi, Gino Bartali and Marco Pantani. In addition to the sporting aspects, the Giro d'Italia has had a significant impact on the social and cultural fabric of Italy, involving entire communities in the celebrations and promoting a sense of national unity.

## 82

### The Human Speed Record on a Bicycle

In September 2019, English cyclist Neil Campbell set a new world record for human speed on a bicycle, reaching a speed of 280.57 km/h.

This extraordinary feat was achieved on a runway at Elvington Airport in England. To reach this speed, Campbell used a specially modified racing bicycle and was towed by a motor vehicle, which allowed him to build up speed before unhooking and pedalling independently.

This record not only showcases Campbell's technical ingenuity and courage, but also represents an incredible example of what is possible in terms of human speed and athletic performance.

## The Altitude Record on a Bicycle

The record for altitude reached on a bicycle was set in 2005 by a team of adventure cyclists. These daring athletes cycled to a height of 8,850 meters on the slopes of Everest, surpassing the previous altitude record.

The climb was an incredible test of physical and mental endurance, faced in extremely difficult conditions, including thin air and intense cold. This feat not only demonstrated the tenacity and courage of the cyclists involved, but also highlighted the human potential to face and overcome extreme limits in challenging environments.

## The Record of Victories at the Giro d'Italia

The Giro d'Italia, one of the most prestigious stage races in the world, has seen some cyclists emerge as true symbols of the competition in its long history. Three cyclists in particular share the record for the most overall victories: Fausto Coppi, Alfredo Binda, and Eddy Merckx, each of whom won the Giro d'Italia five times.

These champions, through their epic feats and legendary rivalries, not only dominated racing throughout their careers, but also raised the level of competition, inspiring future generations of cyclists.

Their victories, achieved through a combination of physical strength, tactical acumen, and mental toughness, have made them iconic figures in the world of cycling and helped define the Giro d'Italia as one of the most demanding and prestigious races.

# 85

## The Longest Cycling Race in One Day: Tommy Godwin's Achievement

In 1939, British cyclist Tommy Godwin achieved an extraordinary feat, completing the longest cycling race ever recorded in a single day.

By covering 561.43 km in just 24 hours, Godwin set a record that has stood for decades as a symbol of exceptional endurance and willpower. This feat was accomplished in conditions that would today be considered extremely primitive, with bicycles and equipment far less advanced than modern standards.

Godwin's finish not only set a cycling world record, but became a landmark in the history of the sport, demonstrating what is possible with determination and physical endurance.

## 86

### Marco Pantani's Alpe d'Huez Climb Record

Marco Pantani, one of the greatest climbers in the history of cycling, set a phenomenal record in the climb of Alpe d'Huez during the 1997 Tour de France. Climbing the 13.8km with an average gradient of 8.1% in just 37 minutes and 35 seconds, Pantani set a time that remains one of the fastest ever recorded on that climb.

This performance has become legendary, not only for the impressive speed, but also for the aggressive style and determination of Pantani, who tackled the famous 21 hairpin bends of Alpe d'Huez with unprecedented grit and speed. His record is still remembered today as one of the most iconic moments in cycling.

# 87

## Eddy Merckx's Record of Victories in the Milan-Sanremo

Eddy Merckx, often described as the greatest cyclist of all time, holds the record for victories in Milan-Sanremo, with seven triumphs in his career. The Milan-Sanremo, known as the "Classicissima", is one of the oldest and most prestigious classic monuments in the world of cycling.

Merckx dominated this race in the 1960s and 1970s, demonstrating unique talent and versatility. His victories in Milan-Sanremo span a variety of racing conditions and strategies, further cementing his reputation as a cyclist of exceptional skill and tactical intelligence.

## Youngest Tour de France Winner: Henri Cornet

Henri Cornet holds the record for being the youngest winner in the history of the Tour de France. In 1904, aged just 19 years and 352 days, Cornet was declared the winner of what was only the second edition of the famous race. His victory was controversial, as it was awarded following the disqualification of several riders for irregularities.

Despite the controversy, Cornet's triumph remains a significant moment in the Tour's history, highlighting the toughness and competitiveness of the race from its early years. His young age and historical context make his victory even more remarkable, considering the difficult racing conditions and length of stages in the early 20th century.

# 89

## Eddy Merckx's unsurpassed record in the Milan-Sanremo

Eddy Merckx, legendary Belgian cyclist known for his countless successes, holds the absolute record of victories in the Milan-Sanremo, one of the most prestigious races in the world of road cycling. With seven triumphs (1966, 1967, 1969, 1971, 1972, 1975 and 1976), Merckx demonstrated an almost unparalleled superiority in this competition, nicknamed the "Classicissima".

Milan-Sanremo, known for its long distance and varied route combining plains, hills and the famous "Poggio di Sanremo", requires a unique combination of endurance, speed, and tactics. Merckx, with his aggressive style and ability to adapt to different types of terrain, conquered this race in several ways, from solo breakaways to powerful final sprints.

## The History of Cycling and the First World War

During the First World War, cycling took on an unexpected and crucial role. Many professional cyclists left racing to join the military, and bicycles became a strategic tool in military operations. Bicycles were used to carry messages, explore, and even transport materials to areas where other vehicles could not reach.

This period also marked a disruption in cycling competitions in Europe, with many races such as the Tour de France and the Giro d'Italia being suspended. However, the resilience demonstrated by cyclists and the role of bicycles in the conflict highlighted the versatility and importance of this medium, which went beyond sport.

# 91

## The Six Day Phenomenon

Six Day races are a unique format in track cycling, originally popular in the United States in the late 19th century. Initially, runners competed individually for six consecutive days, almost without a break, which placed enormous physical and mental demands on them.

Over time, the format changed to become a team competition, with runners taking turns competing. These cycling marathons became famous for the festive atmosphere and entertainment that accompanied them, turning them into popular and spectacular events that attracted large crowds.

## Women in Cycling: Alfonsina Strada

One of the most fascinating figures in cycling history is Alfonsina Strada, an Italian who challenged gender conventions in cycling. In 1924, she participated in the Giro d'Italia, becoming the only woman in history to compete in the race.

Although she was not officially classified due to rules excluding women, Strada completed the race, earning the respect and admiration of her male colleagues and the public. Her participation in the Giro d'Italia not only caused a sensation at the time, but also paved the way for greater inclusion of women in professional cycling.

## The Birth of Cycle Tourism

Cycle touring, the act of traveling long distances by bicycle for pleasure, began to gain popularity in the late 19th century, paralleling the development of cycling as a sport. This form of travel offers a unique way of exploring new areas, combining sport, adventure, and tourism.

One of the first organizations dedicated to cycle tourism was the Italian Touring Club, founded in 1894, which promoted bicycle travel in Italy. Since then, cycle touring has become a global practice, with dedicated cycling routes and itineraries spanning continents, offering cyclists of all levels the opportunity to explore the world on two wheels.

# 94

## The Annual Mileage Record

The annual mileage record held by Amanda Coker in 2017 was an exceptional and enduring cycling feat. Amanda cycled over 86,500km in one year, a distance equivalent to going around the world twice. This record not only required physical endurance and determination, but also detailed planning and constant motivation.

His feat was an example of dedication and commitment in pursuing an exceptional goal in the world of cycling. Amanda had to face daily challenges, manage fatigue, and overcome physical and mental obstacles during her incredible adventure.

## The Evolution of the Cycling Helmet

In 1885, Charles Metz, a well-known engineer and pioneer in the field of cycling engineering, designed and created the first cycling helmet. This original helmet was made of hard leather and was worn primarily to protect cyclists' heads from impacts during their rides.

However, the spread of helmet use among cyclists has been a gradual process. Over the next several decades, helmet designs and materials advanced significantly. During the 1970s and 1980s, as concerns about road safety increased, a greater interest in protecting cyclists began to develop.
It wasn't until the 1990s that the use of cycling helmets became more common and recommended.

## The Altitude Record on a Bicycle

Setting the altitude record on a bicycle was an extraordinary feat that required preparation, endurance and cycling skill. The cycling team, led by Jelle Staleman, took on the challenge in 2005, aiming to reach the highest altitude possible on the slopes of Everest, in an attempt to surpass the previous record.

The expedition required meticulous planning, as the high altitude and extreme weather conditions made the climb extremely dangerous. The cyclists faced extreme temperatures, poor oxygenation, and freezing winds as they attempted to pedal to the top.
The challenge was not only physical, but also mental, as the extreme conditions placed great stress on the body.

# 97

## The Record of the Climb of Alpe d'Huez

The Alpe d'Huez climb is an iconic stage in the Tour de France, characterized by 21 hairpin bends and challenging gradients. In 1997, Marco Pantani set a memorable record during the mountain stage, demonstrating extraordinary cycling strength and skill.

Pantani completed the climb in just 37 minutes and 35 seconds, setting a time that has become a benchmark in the history of the race. His searing acceleration and determination while climbing remains an epic moment in cycling history today, highlighting the exceptional abilities of some riders to master the most challenging climbs.

## The Science Behind Cycling Jersey Design

The cycling jersey is not just an item of sportswear; it is the result of years of research and innovation.

Modern fabrics are lightweight and breathable, helping cyclists maintain optimal body temperature even in the most extreme conditions. Furthermore, the design of a cycling jersey also considers aspects such as reducing drag (air resistance) and optimizing comfort for long distances.

Some jerseys even feature panels of reflective materials to increase visibility during night riding. The science behind these jerseys is so advanced that some teams spend thousands of dollars on research and development to gain even a small competitive advantage.

## 99

### The Psychology of the Lone Cyclist

While many people associate cycling with large groups or teams, there is a less explored but equally fascinating aspect: the psychology of the lone cyclist. Cycling long distances alone can be as much a mental as a physical challenge. Solo cyclists often describe a sense of meditation and introspection during their rides.

We talk about a mental "flow" in which the cyclist finds himself completely immersed in the activity, with a deep concentration that allows him to forget stress and daily worries. This state of mind can lead to significant psychological well-being, as well as promoting creativity and mental clarity. Some solo cyclists use this time to solve complex problems or reflect on important decisions.

## The Environmental Impact of Professional Cycling

While cycling is generally considered a low-impact activity, professional cycling has a less green side. Races such as the Tour de France and the Giro d'Italia involve hundreds of cyclists, support teams, assistance vehicles and fans following the event. This leads to significant fuel consumption and $CO_2$ emissions.

Additionally, high-end racing bikes are often made from materials such as carbon fibre, which have a considerable environmental impact during production and are not easily recyclable. However, there is growing awareness and efforts to make racing more sustainable, for example through the use of hybrid or electric vehicles and the promotion of material recycling.

Printed in Great Britain
by Amazon